This coloring Book Belongs To:

....

ALLIGATOR

B b

BEE

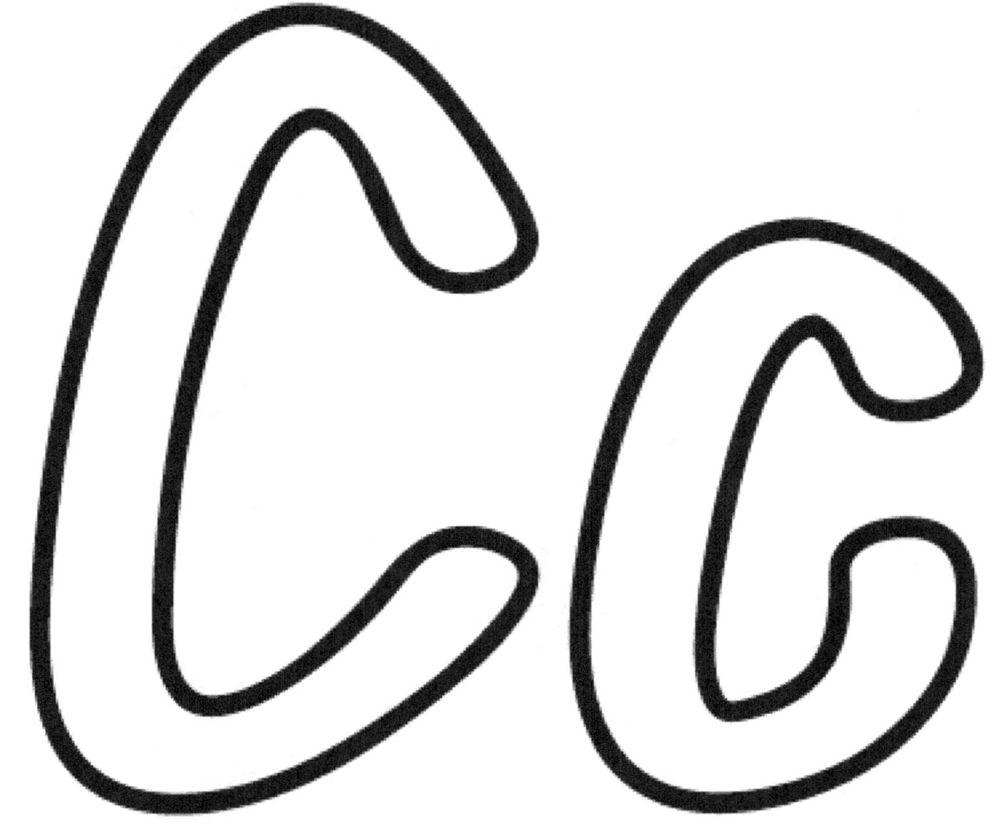

CAT

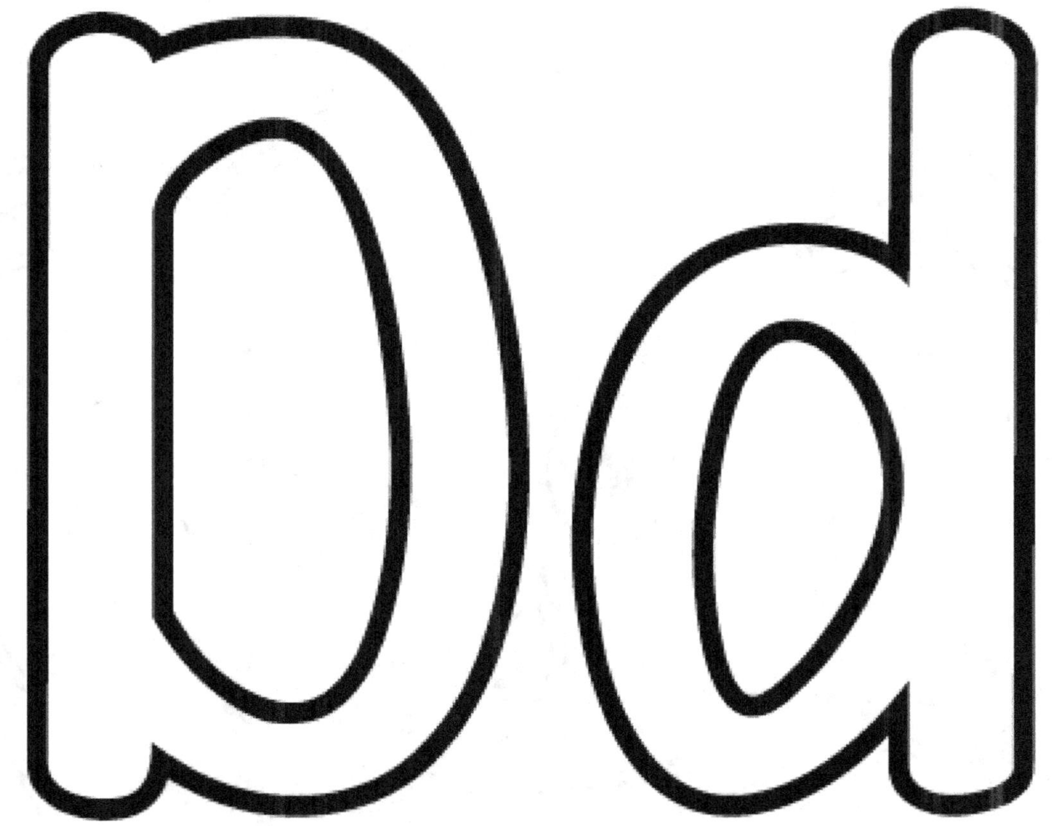

Dd

DOG

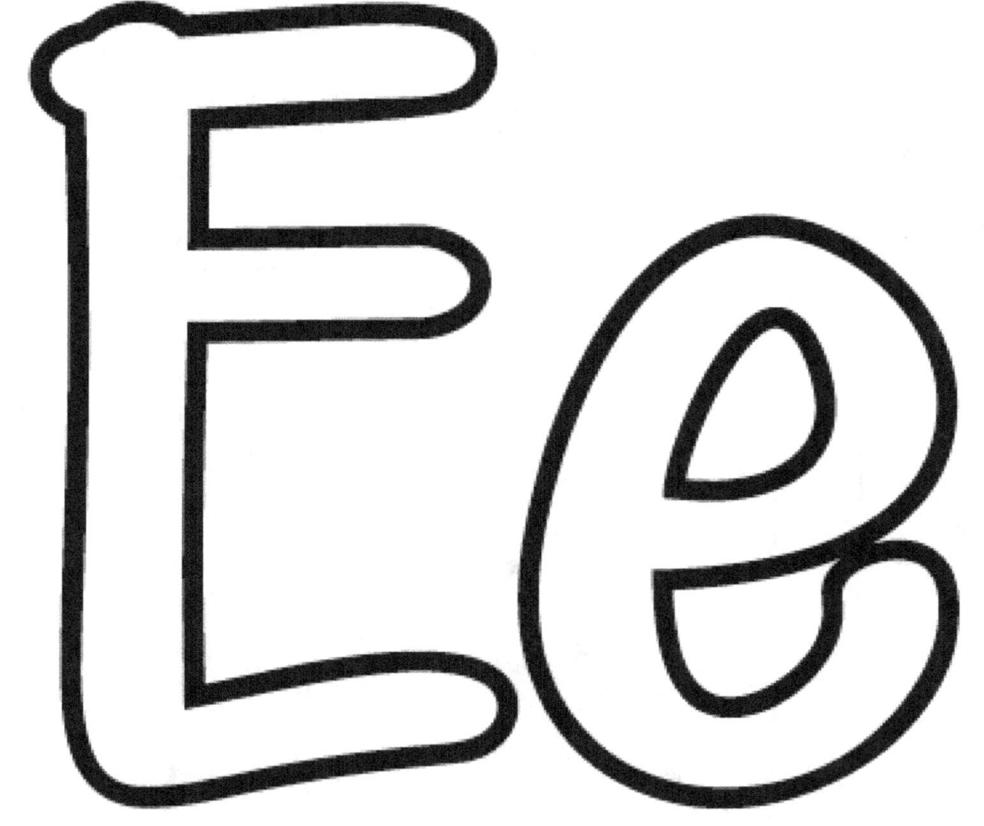

E e

ELEPHANT

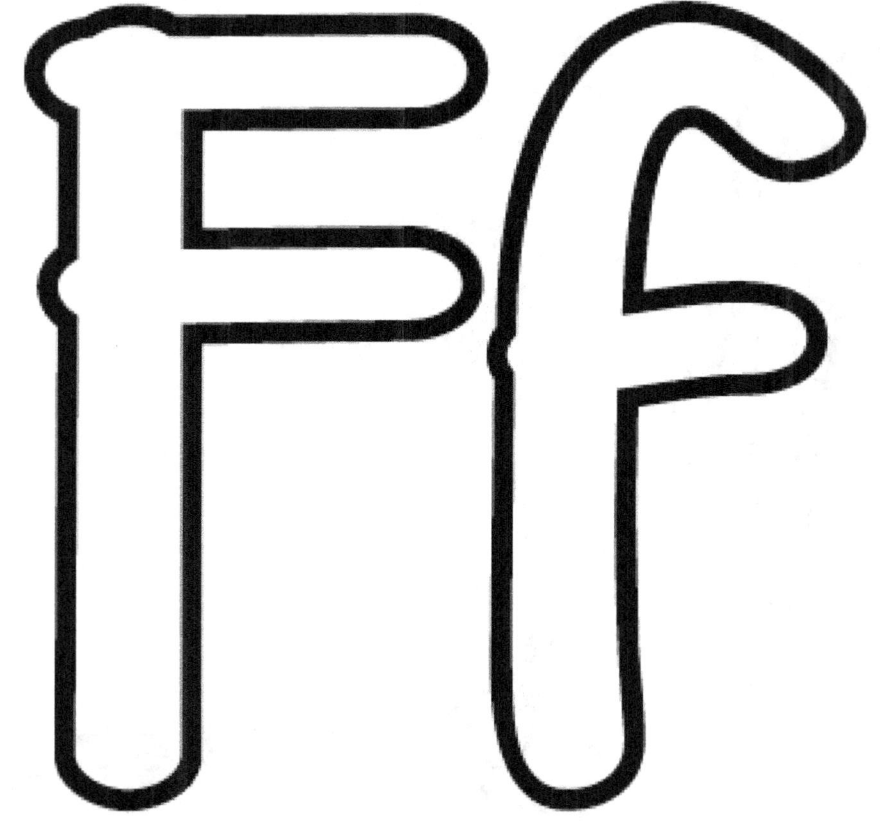

FOX

Gg
GIRAFFE

Hh

HIPPO

Ii

IGUANA

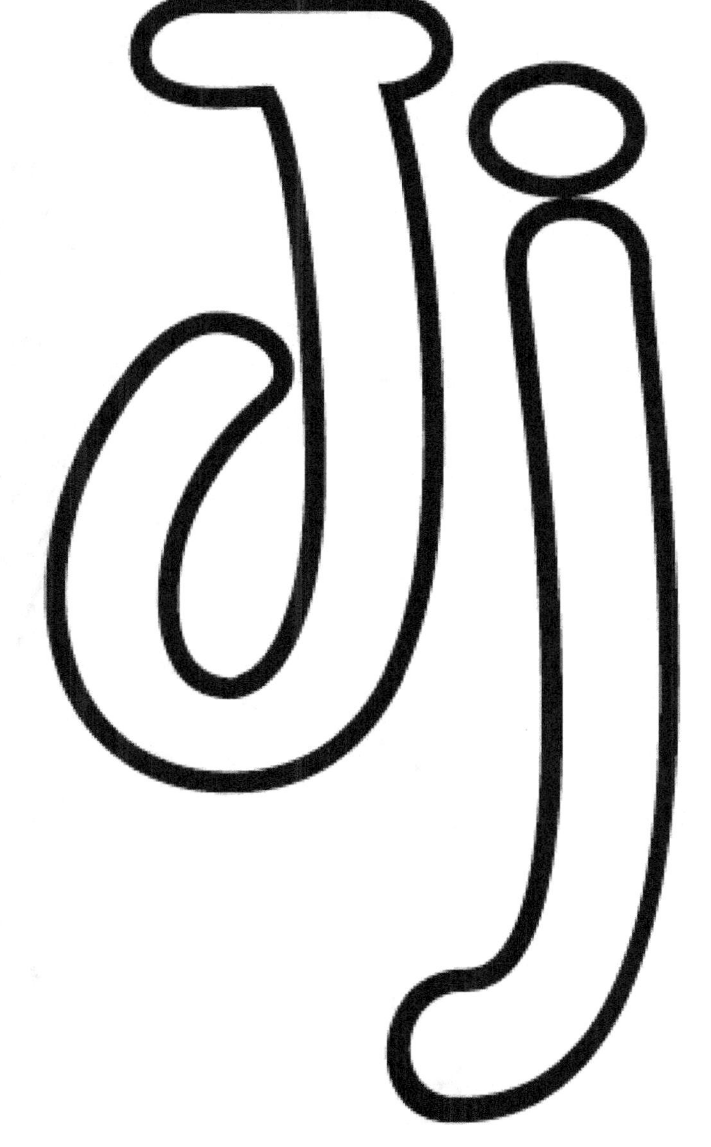

JELLY FISH

Kk

KANGAROO

Ll

LION

Mm

MONKEY

NIGHTINGALE

owl

P p

PENGUIN

QUAIL

Rr

RACOON

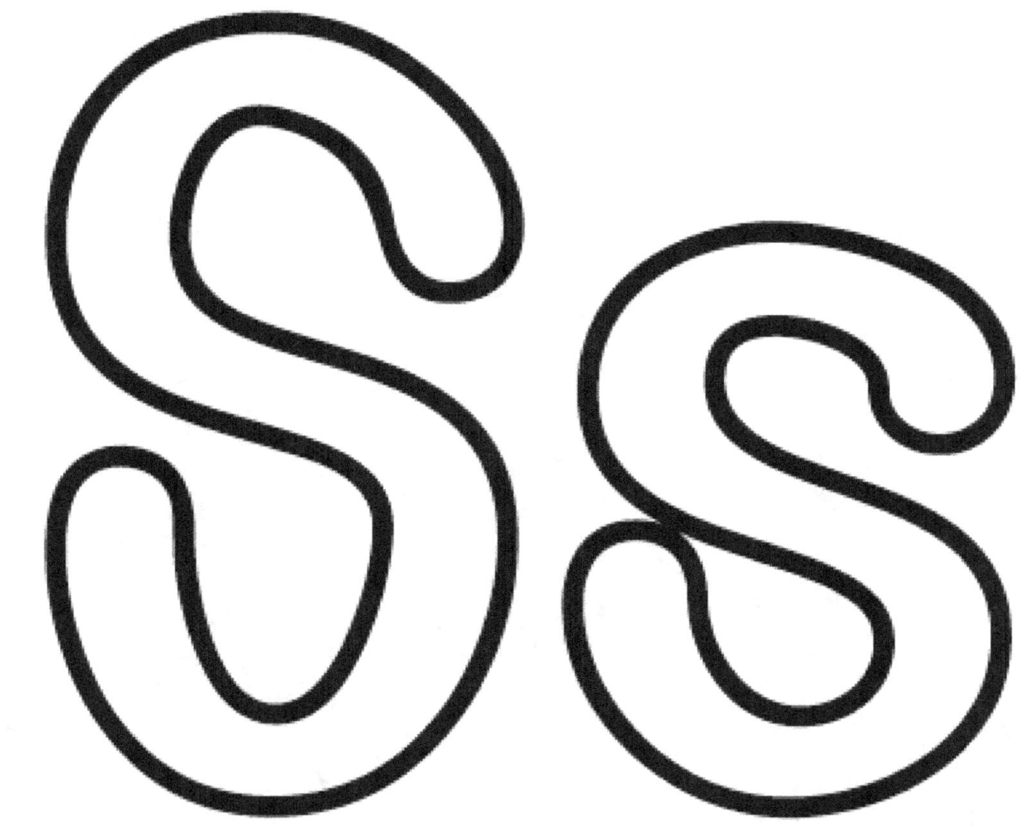
Ss
SEAL

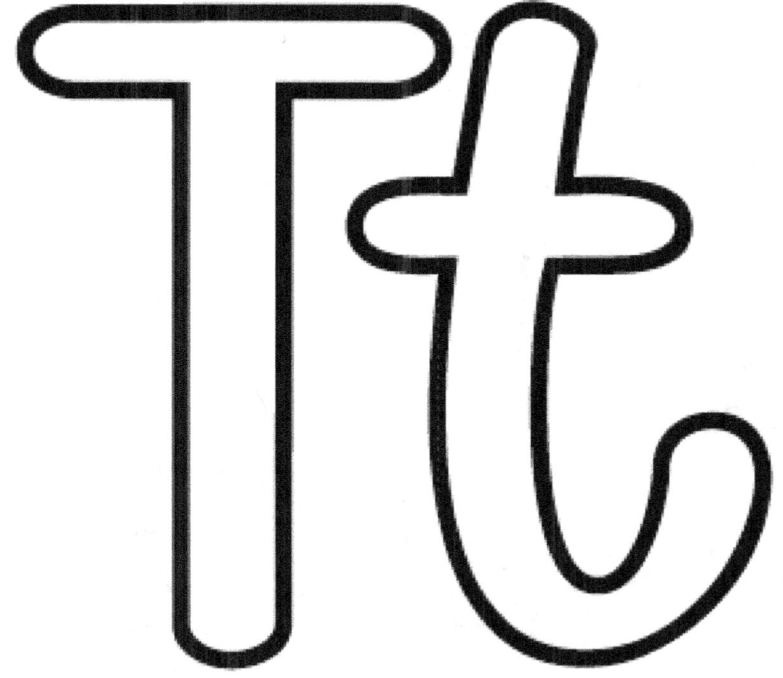

TURTLE

UNICORN

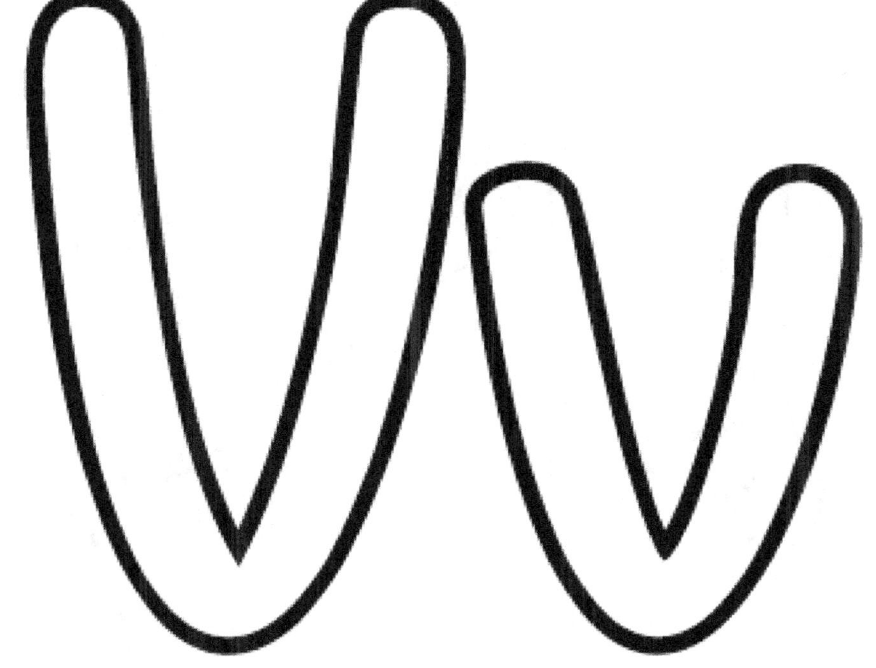

Vv

VULTURE

WHALE

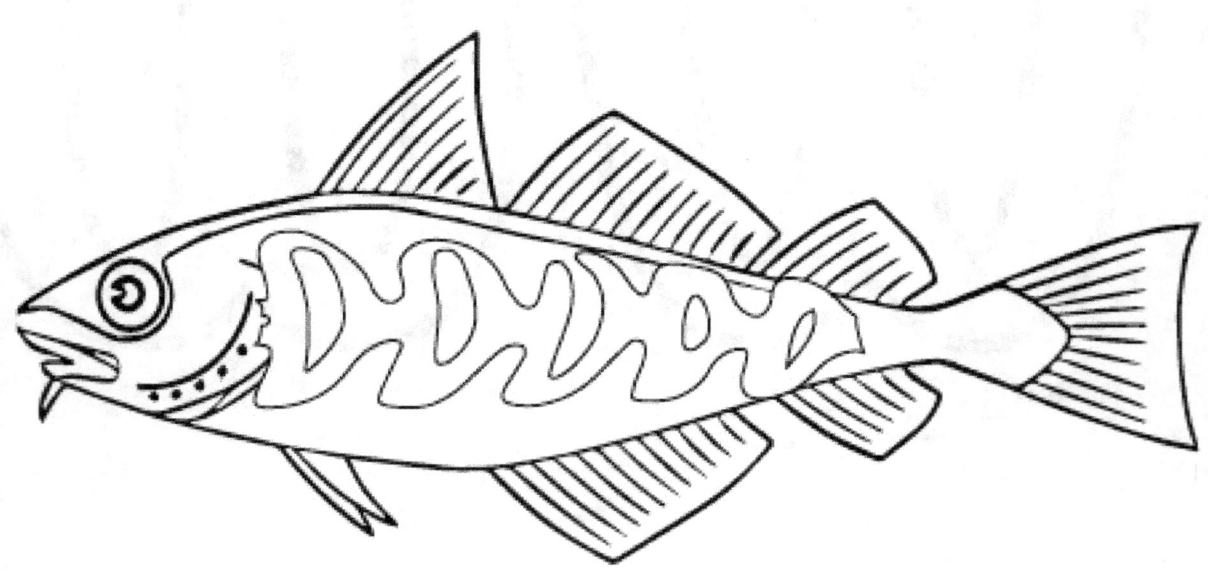

Xx

X-RAY FISH

Yy

YAK

Zz

ZEBRA

Oussa Publisher, 2020

ISBN 9798588168885

https://www.facebook.com/Oussa-Publisher-103909331644015